MLB's Greatest Teams

BOSTON RED SOX

Katie Lajiness

Big Buddy Books
An Imprint of Abdo Publishing
abdopublishing.com

abdopublishing.com

Published by Abdo Publishing, a division of ABDO, PO Box 398166, Minneapolis, Minnesota 55439.
Copyright © 2019 by Abdo Consulting Group, Inc. International copyrights reserved in all countries. No part
of this book may be reproduced in any form without written permission from the publisher. Big Buddy Books™
is a trademark and logo of Abdo Publishing.

Printed in the United States of America, North Mankato, Minnesota.
052018
092018

Cover Photo: Stephen Dunn/Getty Images.
Interior Photos: 33ft/Depositphotos (p. 7); Archive Pics/Alamy Stock Photo (p. 11); Charles Krupa/AP Images
    (p. 17); Darren McCollester/Getty Images (p.28); Dawna Moore/Alamy Stock Photo (p. 15); Duane
    Burleson/Getty Images (p. 21); Elsa/Getty Images (pp. 23, 24, 25); Ezra Shaw/Getty Images (p. 19); Getty
    Images (p. 22); Jed Jacobsohn/Getty Images (p. 23); Jim Rogash/Getty Images (p. 5); Maddie Meyer/Getty
    Images (p. 27); Omar Rawlings/Getty Images (p. 29); Otto Greule Jr/Getty Images (p. 22); Rich Gagnon/
    Getty Images (p. 9); Rob Carr/Getty Images (p. 13).

Coordinating Series Editor: Tamara L. Britton
Graphic Design: Jenny Christensen

Library of Congress Control Number: 2017962666

Publisher's Cataloging-in-Publication Data

Names: Lajiness, Katie, author.
Title: Boston Red Sox / by Katie Lajiness.
Description: Minneapolis, Minnesota : Abdo Publishing, 2019. | Series: MLB's greatest
    teams | Includes online resources and index.
Identifiers: ISBN 9781532115141 (lib.bdg.) | ISBN 9781532155864 (ebook)
Subjects: LCSH: Major League Baseball (Organization)--Juvenile literature. | Baseball
    teams--United States--History--Juvenile literature. | Boston Red Sox (Baseball team)-
    -Juvenile literature. | Sports teams--Juvenile literature.
Classification: DDC 796.35764--dc23

Contents

Major League Baseball

There are two leagues in MLB. They are the American League (AL) and the National League (NL). Each league has 15 teams and is split into three divisions. They are east, central, and west.

The Boston Red Sox is one of 30 Major League Baseball (MLB) teams. The team plays in the American League East **Division**.

Throughout the season, all MLB teams play 162 games. The season begins in April and can continue until November.

4

The Red Sox have two mascots. They are Wally the Green Monster (shown) and his sister, Tessie the Green Monster.

A Winning Team

The Red Sox team is from Boston, Massachusetts. The team's colors are red, navy blue, and white.

The team has had good seasons and bad. But time and again, the Red Sox players have proven themselves. Let's see what makes the Red Sox one of MLB's greatest teams!

Fast Facts

HOME FIELD: Fenway Park

TEAM COLORS: Red, navy blue, and white

TEAM SONG: "Sweet Caroline" by Neil Diamond

PENNANTS: 13

WORLD SERIES TITLES: 1903, 1912, 1915, 1916, 1918, 2004, 2007, 2013

Fenway Park

From 1901 to 1911, the Red Sox played at the Huntington Avenue Grounds. The next year, the team moved to Fenway Park in Boston.

Today, Fenway Park is the oldest MLB park still in use. It can seat nearly 34,000 people. The park is famous for its left-field wall called the Green Monster. It stands 37 feet, two inches (11 m) tall!

The Red Sox brought grass from Huntington Avenue Grounds to Fenway Park in 1911.

Then and Now

Founded in 1901, the Boston Americans was one of the first teams to join the AL. The team name changed to the Boston Red Sox in 1908. This name came from the Boston Red Stockings, the city's first **professional** baseball team.

Jimmy Collins was the team's first manager. He led the Red Sox to its first World Series in 1903. The team went on to win four more **championships** between 1903 and 1918.

Cy Young has won more games than any other pitcher in MLB history. Every year, the top pitcher in each league earns the Cy Young Award.

The 1920s proved difficult for the Red Sox. In 1920, the team traded Babe Ruth to the New York Yankees. This trade marked the beginning of the Red Sox and Yankees rivalry.

After the trade, the Red Sox did not win a World Series until 2004. And, the team won two more **championships** since. The players won one title in 2007, and another in 2013.

Some believe the Red Sox had bad luck after trading Babe Ruth. They did not win a title for the next 86 years.

Highlights

Over the years, the Red Sox have had many star players. Together, these players have won every major MLB award. The team has won eight World Series titles. And, it has scored 13 AL **pennants**.

In 2013, the Red Sox earned the Philadelphia Sports Writers Association Team of the Year Award.

Throughout history, the Red Sox have had many famous moments. The summer of 1967 was the Impossible Dream season. The team had not had a winning season for nearly ten years.

Finally, the team hit a winning streak. It moved from fifth place in its **division** to second place in three months. In October, fans went wild when the Red Sox took the AL **pennant**. The team went to the World Series!

In 2017, Carl Yastrzemski honored the 50-year anniversary of the Impossible Dream.

Famous Managers

Terry Francona managed the Red Sox from 2004 to 2011. He led the team to a World Series title during his first year as manager.

Under Francona, the Red Sox won **championships** in 2004 and 2007. In June 2009, the manager earned his five-hundredth win. He also received five **nominations** for Manager of the Year while with the team.

Under Francona, the Red Sox won 744 games in eight years. He is the second manager in team history to accomplish that many wins.

John Farrell became the team's manager in 2013. That same year, he led the team to a World Series win. For the first time in 95 years, the Red Sox won the Series at Fenway Park.

Farrell managed the AL team in the 2014 All-Star Game. He has been **nominated** for two Manager of the Year Awards while with the team.

In 2015, Farrell found out that he had an illness called cancer. Luckily, he beat the disease.

Star Players

Ted Williams LEFT FIELDER, #9

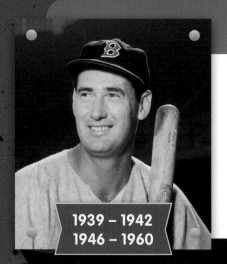

1939 – 1942
1946 – 1960

Ted Williams was with the Red Sox for 19 seasons. He won six MLB batting titles and two **Triple Crowns**. For two years, he led the league in batting average, home runs, and **runs batted in (RBIs)**. He **retired** from baseball in 1960. Six years later, Williams was **inducted** into the National Baseball Hall of Fame.

Wade Boggs THIRD BASEMAN, #26

The Red Sox **drafted** Wade Boggs in 1976. Boggs played with the Red Sox for 11 seasons. Throughout his **career**, he won five AL batting titles. In 2005, Boggs joined the National Baseball Hall of Fame.

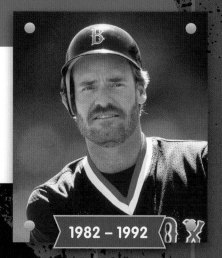

1982 – 1992

Nomar Garciaparra INFIELDER, #5

At 18, Nomar Garciaparra played on the 1992 US Olympic baseball team. He went on to become the starting shortstop for the Red Sox in 1997. That year, Garciaparra won the AL **Rookie** of the Year Award. He **retired** from baseball in 2010.

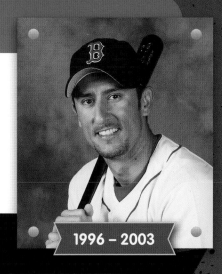

1996 – 2003

David Ortiz FIRST BASEMAN, #34

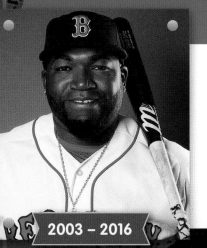

2003 – 2016

David Ortiz, nicknamed "Big Papi," began playing for the Red Sox in 2003. A prized player, he was a three-time World Series **champion**. In 2006, Ortiz earned the Red Sox record for 54 home runs in one season! And, he was named to the All-Star team ten times. Ortiz retired from baseball in 2016.

Dustin Pedroia SECOND BASEMAN, #15

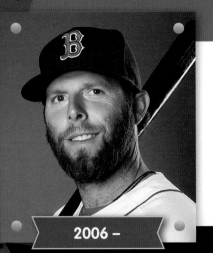

2006 –

The Red Sox **drafted** Dustin Pedroia in 2004. In 2007, he won the AL **Rookie** of the Year Award. The next year, Pedroia became the AL **Most Valuable Player (MVP)**. With the Red Sox, he has won four **Gold Glove Awards** and a **Silver Slugger**. He played on four All-Star teams. And, he helped the Red Sox win two World Series **championships**.

Xander Bogaerts INFIELDER, #2

Xander Bogaerts joined the Red Sox in 2013. Recognized as a standout player, he earned a spot on the 2016 All-Star team. And, he took home two Silver Slugger Awards. He earned one in 2015 and another in 2016.

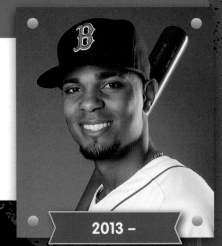

2013 –

Mookie Betts RIGHT FIELDER, #50

Selected in the 2011 **draft**, Mookie Betts joined the major leagues in 2014. The right fielder went on to enjoy much success in 2016. That year, he won the **Silver Slugger** and the **Gold Glove** awards. Betts also played on the 2016 and the 2017 All-Star teams.

2014 –

Craig Kimbrel PITCHER, #46

The Red Sox picked up Craig Kimbrel in 2016. The right-handed pitcher could throw a fastball at speeds of more than 102 miles (164 km) per hour! He has been part of two All-Star Games while with the Red Sox. And in 2017, Kimbrel pitched an **immaculate inning** against the Milwaukee Brewers.

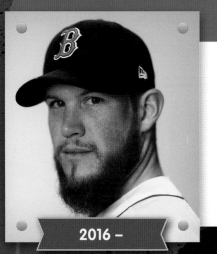

2016 –

Final Call

All-Stars

The best players from both leagues come together each year for the All-Star Game. This game does not count toward the regular season records. It is simply to celebrate the best players in MLB.

The Red Sox have a long, rich history. The team has played in 12 World Series. And it has won eight **championship** titles.

Even during losing seasons, true fans have stuck by the team. Many believe the Red Sox will remain one of the greatest teams in MLB.

Rafael Devers made the team's first postseason, inside-the-park home run since 1916!

Through the Years

1903

The Red Sox beat the Pittsburgh Pirates in the first World Series.

1918

During **World War I**, the Red Sox only played 126 games all season.

1943

Several Red Sox players left the team to fight in **World War II**. Among those was the team's star, Ted Williams. He came back in 1946.

1983

After a 23-year **career**, Carl Yastrzemski played his last game. Fans filled Fenway Park to watch as he received farewell gifts.

1953

The Red Sox scored 17 runs in one inning, setting a new AL record.

1995

Kevin Kennedy became manager. He led the Red Sox to win the AL East **Division** with a record of 86–58.

2004

The Red Sox won the World Series in four games against the St. Louis Cardinals.

2007

The team earned another World Series title. It beat the Colorado Rockies in Game Four.

2017

In 2017, Boston won the AL East Division title for the second straight year.

Glossary

career a period of time spent in a certain job.

championship a game, a match, or a race held to find a first-place winner. A champion is the winner of a championship.

division a number of teams grouped together in a sport for competitive purposes.

draft a system for professional sports teams to choose new players.

Gold Glove Award annually given to the MLB players with the best fielding experience.

immaculate inning when a pitcher throws only nine pitches in a half-inning of play. Each pitch thrown is a strike, therefore striking out three batters in a row.

induct to officially introduce someone as a member.

Most Valuable Player (MVP) the player who contributes the most to his or her team's success.

nominate to name as a possible winner.

pennant the prize that is awarded to the champions of the two MLB leagues each year.

professional (pruh-FEHSH-nuhl) working for money rather than only for pleasure.

retire to give up one's job.

rookie a player who is new to the major leagues until he meets certain criteria.

run batted in (RBI) a run that is scored as a result of a batter's hit, walk, or stolen base.

Silver Slugger Award given every year to the best offensive players in MLB.

Triple Crown the achievement of a baseball player who at the end of a season leads the league in batting average, home runs, and runs batted in.

World War I a war fought in Europe from 1914 to 1918.

World War II a war fought in Europe, Asia, and Africa from 1939 to 1945.

Online Resources

Booklinks
NONFICTION NETWORK
FREE! ONLINE NONFICTION RESOURCES

To learn more about the Boston Red Sox, visit **abdobooklinks.com**. These links are routinely monitored and updated to provide the most current information available.

Index

Wampatuck Media
Center